USING THIS BOOK

*Children learn to read by **reading**, but they need help to begin.*

When you have read the story on the left-hand pages aloud to the child, go back to the beginning of the book and look at the pictures together.

Encourage children to read the sentences under the pictures. If they don't know a word, give them a chance to "guess" what it is from the illustrations before telling them.

There are more suggestions for helping children learn to read in the *Parent/Teacher Guide*.

© Text and layout SHEILA McCULLAGH MCMLXXXV
© In publication LADYBIRD BOOKS LTD MCMLXXXV
Loughborough, England
LADYBIRD BOOKS, INC.
Lewiston, Maine 04240 U.S.A.

Printed in England

When the Magic Stopped

written by SHEILA McCULLAGH
illustrated by TONY MORRIS

Christmas 1986.

This book belongs to:

Mike Shiver

from Grandma

Ladybird Books

One day, Tessa and Tim were
in the garden of the old house.
The wind was blowing the leaves
all over the garden.
Tim and Tessa chased the leaves
for a long time,
but at last they got tired of
that game, and looked around
for something else to do.
"Let's go and see the Magician,"
said Tessa.
"Yes, let's," said Tim.
"I'm sure he's up in the attic.
Come on."

Tessa and Tim
were in the garden
of the old house.

Tim and Tessa climbed up the tree
by the old house.
They jumped down onto the roof,
and ran up to the window.
The window was open.
They looked in.
The room below was empty.

"There's a saucer of milk
on the table," said Tessa.
"Do you think the Magician
left it for us?"

"Yes," said Tim. "Let's go and see."

Tim and Tessa jumped down
onto the roof.
They looked in at the window.

7

There was a pole propped up
near the window.
The two little cats climbed
down the pole. Tessa saw
a label lying on the floor,
with a word written on it.
The word was "No."

"Look," said Tessa. "It says 'No.'
What does that mean?
Do we have to keep off the floor?"

"It can't mean that," said Tim.
"Maybe the Magician dropped it."
They jumped up onto the table.

"Look," said Tessa.

There were two saucers on the table.
One was full of milk.
There was a label propped up
against it.
The word on the label was "Yes."
"It's for us," said Tessa.
Tim and Tessa drank the milk.
It was very good.

"What's the other saucer?" asked Tim.
"It's a flying saucer," said Tessa.

There were two saucers
on the table.

Tim and Tessa looked at
the flying saucer.

"How does it fly?" Tim asked.

"You get in and press that button,"
said Tessa. "Then you wish,
and the saucer takes you
where you want to go."

"Let's go somewhere," said Tim.
"If the Magician didn't want us
to fly it, he'd have put a label on it,
saying 'No.'"

Tim and Tessa looked at
the flying saucer.

The two little cats
jumped into the saucer.
Tessa put her paw on the red button.
The saucer flew up off the table
into the air.
It hovered above the table.
"I wish the saucer would fly,"
said Tessa.

The two little cats
jumped into the saucer.
"I wish the saucer would fly,"
said Tessa.

At once, the flying saucer
flew out the window.
It flew over the garden.
It flew over the houses.
It flew on and on,
till it came to the park.

The flying saucer
flew out the window.

"It's a wonderful saucer!" cried Tim.
He was very excited.
"Can you make it fly any faster?"

"I'll try," said Tessa.
She put her paw on the button.
"I wish to fly fast," she said.

The saucer flew faster and faster.
It flew over the river, and
over the hills.

The saucer flew
faster and faster.

"Look!" said Tim.

"There's a wood over there.

Can you make the saucer

fly over the wood?"

"I think so," said Tessa.

"I wish to fly over the wood,"

she said.

And she pressed the red button.

At once, the saucer flew to the wood.

The saucer flew
over the wood.

It stopped in the air,
and hovered over the trees.
"Make it fly down to the ground,"
said Tim. "We'll explore the wood."

"I wish to fly down to the ground,"
said Tessa.
She pressed the red button
with her paw.
Nothing happened.
The saucer didn't move.
It stayed where it was, over the wood.

The saucer didn't move.

"Why doesn't the saucer fly down?"
asked Tim.

"I don't know," said Tessa.
"I'll try again."
She pressed the red button
with her paw.
"I wish to fly down to the ground,"
she said.

Nothing happened.
The saucer didn't move.
It stayed where it was,
over the wood.

The saucer didn't move.

The sun was beginning to set.
"Maybe we'd better go home,"
said Tim. "It will be dark soon."

"I wish to go home," said Tessa.
She pushed the red button
as hard as she could.
But the saucer didn't move.
It stayed where it was,
over the wood.

The saucer didn't move.

Tessa tried again and again.
She wished very hard,
and she pushed the red button.
But nothing happened.
The saucer stayed where it was.
The sun set, and the stars came out.
The moon came up over the wood.
"I **wish** I was home," said Tessa.

"So do I," said Tim.

"I wish I was home,"
said Tessa.
The saucer didn't move.

Just then a great white bird
came flying up from the wood.
It was a big white owl.
"Who are you?" he called,
as he flew by.
"Who-oo-oo are you-oo-oo?"

"I'm Tim," said Tim.
"And I want to go home."

"So do I," said Tessa.

They both began to meow.
"Meow! Meow!" said Tim and Tessa.

A big white owl flew by.

The owl landed on the edge
of the saucer.
"Have you stolen the Magician's
flying saucer?" he asked.

"No," said Tim.
"The Magician is a friend of ours.
We live in his garden.
We were just out for a ride."

"I should think the saucer
has run out of wishes,"
said the owl.

The owl said, "The saucer
has run out of wishes."

"What do you mean?" asked Tessa.

"The flying saucer runs on wishes,"
said the owl. "When you've had
three wishes, it won't go any farther.
The Magician has to pour in
some magic wishes,
before the saucer will fly again."

"We've had three wishes," said Tim.

"Then that's why it won't go,"
said the owl.

"Then we'll never get home!"
cried Tessa.

"The flying saucer
runs on wishes,"
said the owl.

"I'll take you home," said the owl.
"If you are friends of the Magician,
you are friends of mine.
Jump on my back.
I'll take you home."

"What about the saucer?" asked Tim.

"I'll tell the Magician where it is.
He'll send for it," said the owl.

So Tim and Tessa jumped onto
the owl's back.

Tessa and Tim jumped
onto the owl's back.

Away flew the owl, over the wood.
He flew over the hills,
and over the river.
He flew over the park,
and over the roofs of the houses
in the town.

The owl flew away.
He flew over the roofs
of the houses.

At last they came to the old house
where the Magician lived.

The moon was shining down.

The owl flew down into the garden.

Tim and Tessa jumped off his back.

They were **very** glad to get home.

"Thank you, owl,"
they both said together.

The owl flew down
to the garden of
the old house.

The owl flew off
to see the Magician,
and Tim and Tessa
crept into their home
under the steps.
"Do you remember that label
we saw on the floor?"
asked Tessa,
as they settled down in the box.

"Yes," said Tim. "It said 'No.'"

"I think it must have fallen
off the flying saucer," said Tessa.

Notes for the parent/teacher

Turn back to the beginning, and print the child's name in the space on the title page, using ordinary, not capital letters.

Now go through the book again. Look at each picture and talk about it. Point to the caption below, and read it aloud yourself.

Run your finger under the words as you read, so that the child learns that reading goes from left to right.

Encourage the child to read the words under the illustrations. Don't rush in with the word before he/she has had time to think, but don't leave him/her struggling.

Read this story as often as the child likes hearing it. The more opportunities he/she has to look at the illustrations and **read** the captions with you, the more he/she will come to recognize the words.

If you have several books, let the child choose which story he/she would like.

dropped ...
She made such a noise,
that she woke Mr Gotobed,
who was fast asleep in bed
in the house at the end
of the lane.

Mr. Gotobed woke up.

Have you read the stories in **Stage 1**
about Tim and Tessa and the Magician?

Stage 1

*from
Tim Turns
Green*